Meet the Family
My Brother

by Mary Auld

Gareth Stevens Publishing
A WORLD ALMANAC EDUCATION GROUP COMPANY

This is Emma and her brother James with their mom and dad. James is five years younger than his sister Emma.

Nasser's brother is just a baby. Nasser sometimes holds him.

Heather's brother is her twin. They were born fifteen minutes apart.

Claire and her older
brother David have
different dads.
David is Claire's
half brother.

Steve and Michael are stepbrothers. Steve's mom and Michael's dad are married to each other now, but they had Steve and Michael with other people before they met.

Zoe's brother goes
to preschool.

Andy's brother has
a part-time job.

Li's brother has a computer. He lets Li use it.

Ed likes to do stunts
with his brother.

Sometimes Rachel and her brother wrestle.

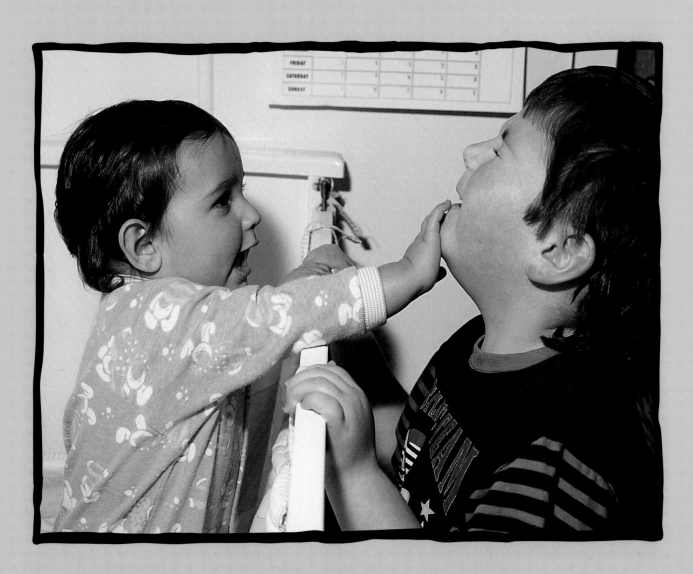

Louise has bike races
with her two brothers.

Molly and her brother build forts in their backyard.

This is Scott with his mom and Uncle Carl. Uncle Carl is Scott's mom's brother.

Do you have a brother?
What is he like?

Family Words

Here are some words people use when talking about their brother or family.

Names for children:
brother, sister, son, daughter.

Names for parents:
father, daddy, dad, papa,
mother, mommy, mom, mama.

Names of other relatives:
grandchild, grandparent,
grandmother, grandma,
grandfather, grandpa,
uncle, aunt, nephew, niece.

A step relative is a person who is related by a parent's remarriage, not by birth.

A half brother and a half sister are related to each other by only one parent.

A Family Tree

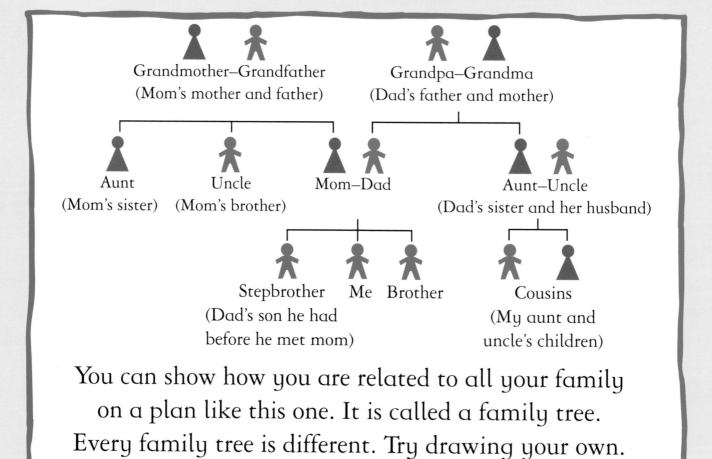

Grandmother–Grandfather
(Mom's mother and father)

Grandpa–Grandma
(Dad's father and mother)

Aunt
(Mom's sister)

Uncle
(Mom's brother)

Mom–Dad

Aunt–Uncle
(Dad's sister and her husband)

Stepbrother
(Dad's son he had
before he met mom)

Me Brother

Cousins
(My aunt and
uncle's children)

You can show how you are related to all your family
on a plan like this one. It is called a family tree.
Every family tree is different. Try drawing your own.

Please visit our web site at: www.garethstevens.com
For a free color catalog describing Gareth Stevens Publishing's list of high-quality books and multimedia programs, call 1-800-542-2595 (USA) or 1-800-387-3178 (Canada). Gareth Stevens Publishing's fax: (414) 332-3567.

Library of Congress Cataloging-in-Publication Data available upon request from publisher. Fax (414) 336-0157 for the attention of the Publishing Records Department.

ISBN 0-8368-3924-2

This North American edition first published in 2004 by Gareth Stevens Publishing, A World Almanac Education Group Company, 330 West Olive Street, Suite 100, Milwaukee, WI 53212 USA

This U.S. edition copyright © 2004 by Gareth Stevens, Inc. First published in 2003 by Franklin Watts, 96 Leonard Street, London EC2A 4XD. Original copyright © 2003 by Franklin Watts.

Series editor: Rachel Cooke
Art director: Jonathan Hair
Design: Andrew Crowson
Gareth Stevens editor: Betsy Rasmussen
Gareth Stevens art direction: Tammy Gruenewald

Picture Credits: Bruce Berman/Corbis: front cover center below. www.johnbirdsall.co.uk: front cover main, 1, 5, 12, 18, 22. Craig Hammell/Corbis: 9. Judy Harrison/Format: 17. Carlos Goldin/Corbis: front cover center above. Sally Greenhill, Sally & Richard Greenhill: 16, 19. Ronnie Kauffman/Corbis: 20. Peter Olive/Photofusion: 13. Gary Parker/Photofusion: 6. Jose Luis Pelaez/Corbis: front cover center top, 14. George Shelley/Corbis: front cover bottom. Ariel Skelley/Corbis: front cover center. Bob Watkins/Photofusion: 11. Lisa Woollett/Format: 2. While every attempt has been made to clear copyright, should there be any inadvertent omission please notify the publisher regarding rectification.

Printed in Hong Kong/China

1 2 3 4 5 6 7 8 9 08 07 06 05 04